Tokaido Road

Nancy Gaffield works as a lecturer at the University of Kent. She was born in the United States and lived in Japan for many years. She currently lives with her husband in Canterbury. This is her first published volume.

'A hugely ambitious and complex project, and the writing is always intelligent and thought-provoking.' – Susan Wicks

東海道

Tokaido Road

Nancy Gaffield

Acknowledgements: With thanks to the writers and readers who
supported me in putting together this work.
Heartfelt thanks to Susan Wicks, Todd McEwen and David Herd.
My love to Maurice Vile.
Had I not met the painter Kurata Tetsu and his wife Nagako,
this book would not have been written.
Some of the poems have appeared in *The Bow-Wow Shop*
(www.bowwowshop.org.uk) and in the anthology *Did I Tell You?:
131 Poems for Children in Need.*

First published in 2011
by CB editions
146 Percy Road London W12 9QL
www.cbeditions.com

Printed in England by Blissetts, London W3 8DH

ISBN 978-0-9567359-0-4

東
海
道

Tokaido Road

Nancy Gaffield

CB *editions*

Acknowledgements: With thanks to the writers and readers who
supported me in putting together this work.
Heartfelt thanks to Susan Wicks, Todd McEwen and David Herd.
My love to Maurice Vile.
Had I not met the painter Kurata Tetsu and his wife Nagako,
this book would not have been written.
Some of the poems have appeared in *The Bow-Wow Shop*
(www.bowwowshop.org.uk) and in the anthology *Did I Tell You?:
131 Poems for Children in Need.*

First published in 2011
by CB editions
146 Percy Road London W12 9QL
www.cbeditions.com

Printed in England by Blissetts, London W3 8DH

ISBN 978-0-9567359-0-4

for Erin

These poems respond to Hiroshige's series of woodblock prints *Fifty-three Stages of the Tōkaidō*. (The prints may be viewed online at www.hiroshige.org.uk/hiroshige/tokaido_hoeido/tokaido_hoeido. htm.) The Tokaido linked the eastern and western capitals, and thus the print series begins at Nihonbashi in Edo (Tokyo) and terminates at Kyoto's Sanjo Bridge. All sorts of people travelled the Tokaido — feudal lords, shoguns, pilgrims, actors, entertainers and tourists. While figures appear in most of the prints, they are never foregrounded, but part of the landscape. The poems foster imaginative links between painting and poetry, capturing the many personae, experiences and memories encountered in the journey.

Contents

1 Nihonbashi

All places exist in relation to Nihonbashi. Everything
begins here. Soft caps of the bay glimmer
in phosphorescent light. The men's breath disappears
into a grove of bamboo. Beneath their feet
stones awaken while overhead the vermilion bird
schooners south. Cursing and grumbling,
sandaled carriers regret the maiden chorus
of farewell, their silken scarves flushed with desire.

Inside, the edo-jin stir ashes to a dogged glow.
A pair of curs sniff the bridgehead and the rat
that passed there, now wallowing unreachable
in river silt. They turn their backsides
to our Hiro as he slips out of sight. The old town
droops into silence and the rains begin.

2 Shinagawa

The bridge shivers with our passing.
Cheek by jowl houses ascend. Light seeps
through the gap between clouds and sea
reminding us that now the fishing's over.
I know I've been here before, know
without looking seven ships bob
on the surface, four trim their sails
before they slip out to sea, unobserved.
Someone reveals his hand: it's the ten of swords.
Nowhere to go but up.

Everything's happening on the roadside:
someone's boiling oden; vendors peddle souvenirs
of Shinagawa. Tea houses rub shoulders with
whore houses. A Tokyo drifter sits in a window
holding a fan, her face painted white with a pair
of heart-shaped lips. I want to tarry
but it is the fullness of time –
someone is waiting.

3 Kawasaki

Hunkering, Hiro abides by the rules,
waits to board at the recess of the river.
Tide hangs back with the ashes
of those who drowned at sea.

He shuffles out of sight. A ferryboat lures
the eye across the Tama, passengers wait
on the opposite bank before a cluster of houses
and a mule laden with barrels of sake.

Close to the distant shore a man on a raft searches
for a hole to cast his line. Hiro boards to cross
the border between this world and under. *If I plunge
into the river here will I quicken?*

Gulls and kingfishers sweep the surface clean of insects,
to the west clouds note the place the sun has pitched up.
All around the muddy marsh twisted pines grasp
for light, one by one rooftops clarify.

Change comes. First the earthquake,
then B29s. These hills
lopped for landfill. He tips the boatman
and wishes he'd stayed home.

4 Kanagawa

Late evening clouds
are stained with indigo.
Minding the eaves
at the roofs' rim,
we heft up the hill.
A ribbon of blue
loops through the sky

TIME IS A CHANGER.

Through a carcass of trees the moon
looms. The seasons seize me too.
Old leaves thrown to earth
blame the tree, but new shoots
return from leavings.
Turn to the sun.

5 Hodogaya

A stream at Hodogaya.
At the bridgehead a toothless fishwife
beckons the travellers
with sweetness. Operatic *irasshaimases*
from soba chefs in clouds
of broth, and then to cap it all
a chorus of slurps.

Satisfied customers.

Kikuyo opens her carriage and steps
out. Monks approach
from the execution grounds,
lure her in to amuse themselves.
A sign pointing to Kamakura reads:

Cultivate the joy of being rather than having.

6 Totsuka

These prints I first saw in Eugene in the spring of 1977. Observe the two-dimensional quality, the flatness of the picture-plane. What is seen is a mirror image. The text or image is drawn onto paper fixed to a piece of cherry wood, and then cut away according to the outline drawing. The carved woodblock is inked, and with the application of paper and pressure, a scene appears. The first of these are indigo but gradually monochrome evolves into brocade. I linger in the picture. Not the scenes of the demi-monde but the landscapes, where 'the individuality of nature is seen isolated from the entire', as Noguchi explained it in 1921. No longer valued after the war, they were borne overseas as wadding. Like them, I am always crossing the water.

Totsuka's neon defeats the stars.
I do not recognise the road
in the print lined with shapely pines,
today concrete stilts
for the railway to DreamLand.

She's there to receive me. *We waited
for you*, she says, guides me in to the alcove,
hands me a stick of incense
to place before his photograph.
We clap hands to summon his soul. She pours
the spring sake, arranges fresh peonies,
his cup overflows.

Remember — all existence is cyclical.
See that we do not lose you.

7 Fujisawa

After Ashbery's 'What Is Poetry'

As Hiroshige views it, a medieval temple with torii, mist settles
over the valley obscuring the houses, no place for blind men.

Tour groups with loudspeakers at the Order of the Wayfarer,
trying to recite *Namu Amida Butsu* for salvation.

The priest of the abandoned says to forsake family, desist
from lust. We are allowed only twelve personal items: rice bowl,

case for chopsticks, winter clothes, surplice, summer clothes
made of flax, handkerchief, sash, washi, string of beads, straw
    sandals,

cowl. Simply repeat the phrase: *Namu Amida Butsu*. The gate
marks transition from the sacred to the profane world, sign-
    posted

Enoshima Shrine where a milk-white nude with eight arms sits
    half-lotus,
female genitals exposed, playing a lute. And to the west a cave

called the womb where the holy one abides. The rare individual
nature reveals in isolation, Hiroshige in us all.

8 Hiratsuka

The road this morning doesn't say much,
it zigzags over water,
nuzzles the wind close to shore.
Picking algae at low tide, sea women scour
the mudflats, hanging it to dry in heavy sea air.
An old woman brushed by age
watches a courier run past
the breast of Mt Koma,
slice Fuji in half.

Now the real world rushes in with force.
I am an old woman seeking
a memory. I carried my daughter.
She rode my hip, heels spurring me
on, there were bruises. I clambered up
to the cave where the hermit lived,
handrailing branches and weeds.
We kept stopping among the wreck
and tangle of roots to listen for cricket-trill.
My breath came hard
as labour. I licked her salty seaweed hair,
caked with dried blood. Up here I was
on the rim of everything. I wanted to stay
until roots tendrilled my ankles, my back
became one with bark.

Instead, I joined the throng on the road
west, even as I heard a voice cry
    creeck   *creeck*

I was careful never to let my reflection play
on water, lest my soul leak out.
Too late. I am an old woman
found by a memory.

9 Ōiso

Rain slashes black lines through a yellow sky at Ōiso. It is spring and I arrive at the haiku house to sit with Hiro at the foot of Tiger Stone. I think of him until a cat comes and circles himself into an O in the corner of the porch. Hiro's woman weeps in the opposite corner; big tears drop onto pages of her, rubbing out words. Her hands fumble her clothes seeking a handkerchief tucked inside the sleeve. It's three in the afternoon, too early to drink, too late to sleep. *I am lonelier than I have ever been*, she tells her companion on the other side. The cat says nothing, no one on the road. Hills, sea, trees – all blackness.

> May 28 and rain heavy as ever on this day
> Tora-gozen lost her lover.*

> Bright coast with sunlight
> travellers flood the road

> Rains surge
> poems return

* The rain falling in this print is significant. Tora-gozen was the 12th-century mistress of Soga-no-juro. The pair killed a government official at Ōiso in order to avenge the death of her father. Her lover, Juro, was killed and Tora herself turned into a stone. Each year the stone is said to weep on the anniversary of Juro's death, and it is believed that the rain on this day is Tora's tears. There is also a famous house where poets come to write haiku here.

10 Odawara

Wide river and no bridge,
the carriers sprout wings,
enter the river avoiding whirlpools
and the threat of drowning.

Choked by a cloud of midges
the men are oiled and plumed.
Carp swoosh between
the spokes of their legs.

The passenger watches
from her cushioned perch, cradles
crickets in a bamboo cage. Inside
her own, a bleating cry.

The river pumps and gathers
speed, toes fathom the contours,
water colours, saffron-veined
mother lode.

Her heart now the weight of a feather,
paradise, but first this long
journey with many gates
to the field of offerings.

11 Hakone

Did the face of the ridge change as we climbed
higher, avoiding the knife edge?
These peaks are unforgiving.

Your outstretched hand sparks
a crackling between us.
I will not let you go.

From the bough of the black pine
the cry of a shrike pierces the sky.
Night advances on the lake below.

Too late to ask
did we have to travel this far.
Path succumbs to thicket, to sedge.

Grey haze shields the valley.
I believe you are just ahead,
I will find you.

12 Mishima

Trees travel in groups, forgetting
their shadows. In morning mist

they resemble strips of black paper.
Horse and rider, like the old

beliefs, have never gone away. Yesterday
we crossed Hakone Pass. Hard going,

no get-out. It's our own fault — we sat up
playing Go under a sky brimming with

reflected Sirius, woke to a world of silence
and mist. Everything arbitrary,

like the mature geisha in a bad economy —
if only Townsend Harris had stayed home.

But oh no he just had to come, see and pry
the monster open, swallow it whole — pearl and all.

Horse and rider emerge from the mist.
Hiro's heard the women of Mishima are beautiful

but take too much time with their make-up.
53 steps to Dharma.

13 Numazu

The kanji says a pilgrim bound for Kompira
walks beside Kano River. On the farthest shore

a curtain of trees guards Yamabushi tengu, forest
goblin who speaks without moving his lips.

Regret and departure. Sleeves soaked in tears.

I walk forward turning round, like the pilgrim
who carries a mask on his back. A votive gift

for the guardian of seafarers. Harvest moon rises,
kindles the gauze of my dress. Ashes swirl

through trees. I sweep the garden clean of leavings,
count fireflies as they glide from trunk to trunk, contemplate

the surety of things, one thousand eight hundred sixty-eight
    steps
to the small shrine at the top where Hiro is now.

14 Hara

Eighty miles from Edo, Fuji's peak escapes
the picture frame, squats shadowless
above a plateau of over-ripe grass.

Nothing but white light and the thin scream
of cranes ascends through a window to
a liquid world, a delicate day,
two women travelling alone.

Half-asleep clouds in an overcast sky,
and long tufts of September grass brush the blue
silk of her dress. They are going nowhere,
cranes too just hanging around.

A sudden chill on the nape says time
to walk on. Somewhere a lone wolf
lopes through the reeds. *Wolves are patient*
remarks one crane to the other.

The breeze shakes loose the folds of her
kimono, a pale blue thigh, bedewed. *Let's wait*
for the wind to drop, lie down
in the long grass and amuse ourselves.

We are miles from anywhere.

15 Yoshiwara

Three riders atop one horse leave Hara in a blizzard
of seed and insect. At mid-morning they pass daimyō
wives held hostage by the shōgun tearing pine bark
with their fingernails. A web straddles the path,
orb-weaver hangs at the hub. Buddha in the undergrowth
measures the distance to Yoshiwara.

Hato bus, old dream-maker, halts before the bridgehead;
travellers order oolong tea, show photos
of Fuji framed by snow-clad pines, Fuji topped with new
moon rising. I find the bus stop named Hidari Fuji
in the kink of the road, no Mt Fuji, just a factory
and a mansion where Fuji should be.

Travellers on the Tokaido
meander between
centuries. Fuji doesn't change.

16 Kanbara

I cross the border of snow at night,
breathe in the picture.

Winter stars coalesce with snowflakes,
station hushed by snow,

a figure under a half-opened umbrella
follows footsteps down the slope.

A shutter opens on an old man crazy
with painting. Summer evening

succulent with crickets and the peonies'
perfume. She sits in the doorway, her kimono

akimbo, indigo butterflies on white linen long
to flee to the safety of flowers; she tries

not to move, her eyes reveal nothing,
but in failing light he intercepts

the wildness in her. A sudden gust of wind
disturbs the distance between us.

The shutter closes on three figures
in the foreground dressed in snow.

17 Yui

At Yui, travellers had a choice: risk drowning at sea or death by bandits
    on Satta Pass. In the garden this morning kill-fish lap
    their bowl indifferent to crows balancing on the rim.
    Ack-ack-ack-ack, crows laugh as they watch fish loop-the-loop.

Kikuyo shivers thinking of travellers peaky as an August moon,
    too close to the edge, torn between safety and danger.
    Trees fall away from the blue-green waters of Suruga,
    four junks head for the point of vanishing.

A grey thought clings to the ledge. He has forgotten. *I am not jealous,*
    though I know he's not alone, Kikuyo thinks. She paints
    her bottom lip and chooses the high road. Leaves
    at once as clouds unravel the day.

18 Okitsu

Fit for service four men ford the river at Okitsu,
bearing sumō and sputtering

yoisho

yoisho

yoisho

Water soothes aching legs. The one they carry,
Man Mountain, sits with folded arms, satisfied
smile, the other on his horse gazes out to sea.

Tonight they will enjoy a good soak with maiko,
trained to rub shoulders and loins,
accomplished in the art of shampooing.

19 Ejiri

Miho peninsula pushes into Suruga Bay,
white sand treads the heels of ancient pines.

The feather mantle flutters and quivers
about her shoulders

yellow lustrous as the full moon at perigee
illumines wave-lap, shadows pines

orbed by a waning moon,
a pair of herons rise east towards Hara

now a crescent as waves recede,
geese fly backwards and fall into the sea

new moon and darkness, clouds part
to show a globe of light.

I am ablaze for you

•

On a sea flecked with lanterns
Nakuryo joins his friends to fish by firelight.

A yellow feather falls from his sleeve.*

* In the Noh play 'The Feather Mantle' (Hagoromo) a fisherman finds a magic
feather mantle belonging to a spirit ('tennyo'). The tennyo demands its return, for
without it she cannot fly back to heaven. He finally agrees, if she will dance for him.
The dance is symbolic of the phases of the moon, and in the finale she disappears
like a mountain that is slowly covered in mist. Today's visitors to Miho no Matsub-
ara can see the 650-year old pine where the five-coloured kimono was discovered.

20 Fuchū

Who's this moving towards me?

Men and horses entering the river's belly.

Away from the bank we see
sweetfish feast on waterweed,
clear water.
The current butters us up,
lures us in.

Mind my weft and I will let you pass.

The river churns,
we shamble through silt where eels spawn,
reeds ribbon our ankles,
we don't fall.

Out here feels different,
mauve changes to green,
it's hard to swim,
fish swish —
we twist to grab hold,
she slips away.

Trust me to steer you clear of the shuttles.

Slick as newborns
we scuttle up the bank,
crawling mewling shaking off
spume, glad for land,
sad for what we've left behind.

21 Mariko

A rush hut shelters beneath
a rose-coloured sky,
weather-worn stones lead up
to yam broth amidst young leaves.
Not one to brood, Mariko straps
the baby to her back, makes ready
for the travellers coming soon.

Here is the dewy path
to leave our cares behind,
Hiro says as he hands her a single
camellia. She bites the head
off, places the stem in a vase,
petals beneath. One time,

one meeting. A wooden well,
bamboo lid, tabi slide
across tatami, water
simmers, tap
of tea spoon, whisking.
Hiro tastes the tea with his ears,
Mariko enjoys the privilege
of service. *The tea is very nice*,
he wipes the lip of his cup once
with two fingers,
places it upside down.

Plum tree bursts into blossom.
Ah, this floating fleeting world!

22 Okabe

Kikuyo enters the defile at nyubai,
the start of the rainy season

> *Is the one I love alive*
> *out there?*

Crow answers
> *Skraww*

Road contracts in the cleavage of Okabe pass,
ivy scrolls up trunks, throttles light

Tengu turns up in the bones
of the hillside,
wind combs the pines
sets needles spinning

> *I know where you are*
> *there floating in air*

Deep in the forest
high up the mountain
iris bloom
the road thickens
with maple branch and vine
traveller with the mask
on his back

Is the one I love
up here somewhere?

Wood thrush replies   *kiskadee*
kata kata kee

23 Fujieda

Then it rained. Not a soft spring rain
but a hammering, bad weather.

May rains, swift current,
no crossing Oikawa

Tokaido black spot.

Rain throbs on, river
breathes – *no one even knows*
I have a story to tell.

> *My fish have lovely fins,*
> *they rarely flounder.*

Rice-paper skin glows
iridescent copper and gold.

> *My fish are coy.*

Their long whiskers tremble
as they brush the naked flesh
of men carrying men.

> *I am patient,*
> *my fingers spread*
> *across the plain*
> *reading you.*

24 Shimada

At last the day dries out,
travellers delirious
to be on the river again.

The river scrambles and splits,
breechclothed coolies flex muscles,
manganese herons follow
runnels, fracture the surface
and come up clean.

I want you to connect the image
with the human story.

Wide and treacherous, water waist-deep
and rising —
daimyō in palanquin, samurai
on a litter, peasants piggy-backed.

> *Lose your footing now*
> *and you are mine, I*
> *will take you away to Suruga Bay.*

Anyone could see the shōgun was beaten.
Anyone could see bridges would be built.

25 Kanaya

You are never far from my thoughts.
I remember you on your raft of oleander
and chrysanthemum, women weeping
on the banks, I soaked the hems of their silks,
carried you from Totomi Bank
to my depths
we lay down together
you were mine at last.

I am a remnant
river, I remember.

26 Nissaka*

She follows the road, it lists above bamboo,
tea plantations, mist and blue mountains.

Every stone covered in moss,
left-over rain drips,
pools. Knit one
purl one. Smell of rotting.

Sound of branches breaking
in the wood dense with cryptomeria
dark as woad.

> *Who's there?*

Thwack of blade
and blood scythes
from the wound, black rain
streams, covers
tree and stone.

Bamboo and tea trees witness
a birth and a death,
say nothing.

An owl with one eye open
sighs, heads fall.

> *I am wanting to speak to my mother
> but my mother is dead*

The hills sag in bewilderment.

> *I am looking for my mother*
> *but she has disappeared*
> *I mourn my mother*
> *from the day I am born*

* The print's subtitle is 'Sayo amid the mountains'. The legend tells of a birth at night. At this spot a robber attacked and killed a pregnant woman who had stopped to rest against a stone. A passing Buddhist monk rescued the newborn child. Years later, the murderer took his sword to be mended, boasting to the swordsmith about how he had killed the woman and damaged his sword. The swordsmith, the murdered woman's son, took his revenge. The ghost of the woman lives in the stone; it wails each night.

27 Kakegawa

High-flying kite breaks
through the edge,
lift greater than weight,
silk and bamboo held
by an invisible hand
and pushed upward

Women stoop in a row of nnnnns,
the mud sucks them down,
they plunge on,
insert the shoots one by one
before blue water hems them in

A child stands with wind
at his back,
unreels string
oops! another kite
escapes the frame,
wind takes it over Mt Akiba,
tengu smiles

Five figures on the bridge
hold onto their hats,
lean into it

A day so beautiful
feels like an absence

That's May for you
everything still
within reach

28 Fukuroi

sits on a plain.

Wayside shelter, June afternoon
tea kettle hangs from tree branch,
water begins to boil.
Travellers stop for a smoke,
a woman stirs the ashes,
desolate and uncomfortable heat.

Perched on a road direction post
wood thrush sings

    kiskadee
        kata kata kee

Outside the picture frame
a garden with seven hundred cherry trees
and the temple of good fortune.
Two benevolent kings guard the gate:
gape-mouthed Agyō heralds
AH for new beginnings,
zip-lipped Ungyō grunts UNH.
Death has the last word always.

Each winter strong winds gather here,
they say it's a good place for kite flying.

29 Mitsuke

I

Mariko's reach always exceeded her grasp,
she couldn't get him
out of her mind. Sure
she got out of bed each morning,
boiled rice, tea,
tried to eat, drink.
Rice stuck in her craw,
she looked in the mirror,
a pelican looked back.
She started to lose weight,
hair, other maiko
kept their distance.
Her insides felt like soba,
nothing connected,
the lump in her throat
moved to her belly.
Hiro didn't return.

II

Two boats moor on a sandy bank,
distant shore draped in mist.
Down-at-the-mouth tour guide
waits with his group,
no glimpse of Fuji today.
Heavenly Dragon River sulks,
chatters with the ferryman.

> *It's time. Come on*
> *in, the water's fine.*

Ahead, Hiro accompanies the sun,
swallows the blame.

30 Hamamatsu

Pine trunk draws a line
down the middle of the print,
halfway mark between Edo and Kyoto.

It's not random
but kind of nearly random
Tokaido, life in miniature.

Man with the pipe stands
apart, smoke funnels
round flame.

Four carriers rub their hands
by the fire, so many selves
unspoken

I am the father flying the kite on my first son's birth,

I am the monk entering the cave to search,

I am the kago bearer raising the arms that hold,

I am the traveller nearing the end of the road.

31 Maisaka

Sea and lake now cut

Edges singe as water changes
from indigo to orange.
I emerge in morning light
resolved
to stand up to this place.

The sea dissolves to a lighter
hue, beneath the water
a shoal of fish,
synchronicity.
I feel them sluice
through my veins,
they ply me with sweets

        Open wide
I do.

The creatures in this place
talk in tongues.
I eavesdrop on their conversations
pick up the odd word
or two

        abunai
        gaijin
        da!

I'll take each title
and tell my own story.

32 Arai

We reach the barrier at midsummer.
Day of the Ox, time to eat eels,
to endure the blaze of August.

Watching him doze on the end of the punt,
more than anything I want to interrupt
his sleep, to fish him from his dream.
I dip my hand in brackish water,
extract an oyster. He sucks out
the sweet flesh in a single gulp.

I lie on tatami watching the sun gild the mist,
the lake comes like a wave.
Most of all I long for your hands
as you wake me from sleep
touching my breasts, my belly,
that tiny pearl, too delicate
for daylight.

Now no one comes
to my bed. I rest my muzzle
against glass until the scene
blurs. Each year at the Day of the Ox
I return to the place where we met.

No one can tell me where this will end.

33 Shirasuka

Someone has removed
all the dustbins
ash heaps
and excrement.

Pine branches balance the left and right sides, the eye of the ob-
server trails down the slope toward the middle of the print. From
right to left a procession leads into the valley. The picture divides
neatly into two: all the greenery and human interest in the fore-
ground, broad and open expanse of sea, immaculate beach behind.
Feudal lords dressed for travel form another element of the land-
scape. Walking hats, no face, they represent themselves by shape.

Who is making? Who is speaking? I shuffle crab-like across the
surface, lamenting my poor facility with Japanese. Who is Hiro?
A painter? A lover? Whose time does he inhabit? And the women
who love him? His is a history with no regret.

Seduced by travel
Hats process down the hillside

Lines run out of time

34 Futakawa

Two bright sparks pass stone jizō
dressed in a red bib.
Ahead a tea house and sweetness
wrapped in oak leaf,
fare for the passage to Sanjūsangendō
and its thousand Buddhas,
each with forty arms to hold you.

That girl digging in the dirt is me.
She pulls herself apart one section
at a time till she is broken
free. A bad-luck year,
thirty-three for women.
Of all the stations on the old Tokaido
this is the bleakest.

What I dreamed of always was this road.

35 Yoshida

Even in my sleep
the river is always there,
river after river
takes shape,
herds us like cattle
across the flood plain.

So many souls
hide their hurt in the hold,
folded into the rift
between marl and flow.
I see them veiled
in blue membrane
and swimming for the surface
plummy, overripe.

Fear drains into my pillow.
Sometime before dawn
my bed settles into river,
shudder of shingle
fast returns the tide
a few more breaths
and I am lost
to tide-flow.

Grim freight tomorrow
in the crook of the river.

36 Goyu

Kikuyo stands at the window
holding her chin up,

she gazes out at the street
ignoring the punters' cries for help.

Inside a room of nuptial paulownia
Obasan washes someone's feet,

a flight of stairs with drawers in the risers
leads nowhere.

A kitchen with a deal table
holds all matter of things –

leeks, laver, a bulbous
daikon, fragrance of fermenting.

Remove your sentiments
and leave them outside the door.

You are never more at home
than when you are here.

37 Akasaka

There is always a river, a lake, the sea: a crossing through water, over a bridge, a tortured pine sometimes covered in snow. A road, setting out, places abandoned. Some remembered.

Wandering and observing the landscape, travellers follow a route, encounter obstacles, make choices, progress.

This time however the artist foregrounds a sago palm in the court-yard. It just fits. An interior scene, doors open. A cupboard stacked with futon. Black hair drifts.

Geisha apply their make-up, a man returns from his bath. A pair of legs descends the stairs.

> *Give me your hand and*
> *I will be*
> *anything you want.*

38 Fujikawa

Outside town a ferryman with a blue
tattoo squats in a hedge of ajisai.
He bends over to pick one,
cartwheels through the door
and lands on the floor,
Thud. The future only half-assured.

July has only begun, and already
the fields have changed to amber.

Like the others I sit with my legs folded
under, forehead bang-on-brick.
The cramp starts in the arch,
writhes upwards and emerges
in wet mascara. I try flattery
till eventually the foot goes numb,
hangs there like blancmange.

Even the cats have bowed down for the shōgun.
No one notices
the artist rendered there.

39 Okazaki

Many crossings, sometimes a bridge. Edge-to-edge, the longest bridge on the Tokaido. Water showcases girders. The eye level with the hills. A procession passes bearing a crest with 38 ravens surrounding an equal number of out-facing arrows. Everyone is going to Okazaki Castle.

In Egypt the pharaohs were laid to rest with 38 cat guardians, 38 ankhs. In 1888 a clowder of 300,000 mummified cats was discovered, ground up and sent to England to be used as fertiliser. The Egyptians killed whoever put a cat to death.

If I had only stayed in Japan. But I wanted to grab the world by the scruff before my neck turned to crepe. Road-struck. Because it could take me somewhere. Different, but never home.

Mariko removed the mote from my eye. Like an amulet I carried her. In the desert her star shone bright. The river bore the pretty worm that kills. I lick my skin to get rid of the smell of the place.

40 Chiryū

April, the pasture flows
with long grass and horses.
Why can't we go on like this for ever?

Horses prick up their ears, invent
their next journey,
how it will change things.

Those men colluding under the tree
mean nothing, I yearn for the sea
today coated in quicksilver.

Each of us has a price
on our heads, we are not the same
as when we started all those rivers ago.

The sea brings armfuls of dulse,
a prospect that whatever happens to others
needn't happen to me. Forget

November's darkening tale,
leap into seafoam. It's a day for wading
through waves, for swimming until myself ceases.

41 Narumi

Down the bank, reeds uncouple,
Hiro disappears like a flame in sunlight.

Kikuyo stays behind, curled into a round ball,
Licking her wounds.

•

Cloth ripples, scene changes.
Arimatsu. Trays arrayed
with storm shibori
blue beyond blue.
Long after you
these hold the shape, scent
of you, until a great wind comes
and irons out the creases.

Roused by the lap of a wave,
the promise of a river,
so many crossings,
you can't remember
all that has happened.
Yes, you've come that far.

42 Miya

A horse and men chasing it.
Perpendicular lines on the right
suggest a shrine at festival time.

All the action takes place
in the centre of the field.
Under a piebald sky the men abandon

themselves to tug-of-war.
I enter their world,
play the game.

Parallel plumes of smoke
rise from the corner,
women shelter

behind wood and silk.
The naked one absorbs
bad luck and evil deeds.

I breathe in the brume.
The men pull back, surge through,
Noli me tangere.

Enter the frame and you're tempted to stay,
too long and you fray the boundary
between semblance and reality.

If you are lucky you will penetrate the place,
lay your hands on the sword of billowing clouds,
though it will not bring you joy.

I'm part of this now.
Follow me to the bridge, I'll show you
the way out.

43 Kuwana

I look for the golden flame
on the bank of the Kiso River.
The boat takes us
to a tea house,
wooden floors polished
by repetitions.

Here the sake tastes of flowers,
over the ayu
we put our differences aside.

I look for you in a poem
but find only unendingness,
imagine a day so light
even memories float away.

I look at your name written on card
in your own hand, the number I call
and call but no one ever picks up.

44 Yokkaichi

I bring myself back to the picture –
a willow anchors the centre
a hat rolls along the jetty
a man chasing it;
soon it will fall out of the frame
(bottom left). My eye shunts to a figure,
arms pinioned, his cloak billows
against a sky of zinc.

This is a good place to die.
I have brought myself back across decades.
Upriver little boats moor amongst benevolent reeds,
news bulletins warn of the coming storm.
Some take heed but there's always a fool
who stands on a jetty facing it.
Take me, I'm yours.

I thought I had finished with the little
danchi on the plain, but I bring myself back,
leaning into the head wind
to get inside. We unrolled
the day, drank absinthe under glass
marked 'X'. It was nice
like a holiday, bunking off.
Even when the hurricane's eye
spied our bed we felt safe
from the peril
ten years ahead.

I reach out to touch you and darkness bleeds
from my fingertips. Never would I have
thought to return here
but I bring myself back
to the same street on the same date
and someone I have never met
opens the door. I catch
a glimpse of an old woman
in the mirror at his back.

45 Ishiyakushi

Yakushi Buddha
holds his right hand in mudra,
sun and moon, his caretakers.

In the canopy crickets sing
a lament of summer's passing.
Sun going down backlights mountain,
birds ribbon lapis-lazuli sky.

Garbed in grey I anchor
on the bank of a shallow river,
an egret settles next to me.
We both stare ahead,
always travellers
in a foreign place.

Those we've left never change.

We talk until the belling
of a temple returns through trees.
When it comes to leaving
you birds are the experts.
Egrets scatter like leaves.

At Ishiyakushi, Buddha of Healing
tells you not to fear.

Moon sweeps the path clean.

46 Shōno

Low cloud confounds the yews,
rain riffles robes,
chimes off stones,
oxidises the mountain
bars on the road.

We had taken a wrong turn.
No one wants to arrive
after dark.

Steam rises from us,
hovers above houses.
Resignation
spills from collars,
trickles down necks,
goads us
on to Tojimbo

    Yoisho
        Yoish o

Tree elders topped in grey
watch us run our course.

The stone ahead
becomes the headstone.

47 Kameyama

No smoke trails from the chimneys,
everyone's asleep. Hiro walks with the howling wind
and fast-flowing clouds to a different world.

A crane with silver wings glances back,
urges him to follow. In Kameyama's yard
many tombs buried in deep snow.

A small party reduced by a grey and mangy sky.
No sound but the travellers' panting and coughing,
they clutch at tufts of wind.

Hiro gutters, out of sorts, mumbles something
disagreeable to his companion;
crane changes course, disappears over trees.

It would be easy to sink down under a thick fleece
until your last breath shimmers.

A woman sits alone on a temple porch.
Snow is falling.

48 Seki

Blue, blue is the sky
indifferent to my pain.
I have travelled far
to see him again,
told he died
last winter.

His ashes mulch the sakura.
I am given a shawl
dyed with their blossoms.
This is not
what I wanted
this is not it
at all.

Why bother to brush my hair?
I'll live out my days
in aimlessness,
close and lock the gate,
let the knotweed take the rest.

49 Sakanoshita

The painter throws his brush
in a fit of pique.
Jun ken po
I cannot show,
mountain wins.

Clear streams cover mossy
stones in cobalt green.
That old fugitive, time
skulks in the shadows,
waits for the brush to fall.

A flock of herons
skein through schist,
scent the sea and know themselves
to be blue water.

Observers at the edge
toss pebbles to judge
where land meets ravine.

Kano Motonobu's ghost
slides through eel grass,
owl in the larches
murmurs *hoooo*

50 Tsuchiyama

The cinereous sky knows the hour
of the sun's setting but isn't saying.

There is a river near here
where she walked one day

filled her pockets with flint
and stepped in.

As if into a lightless room,
she reached out her hands

and grasped the hollowness.
I gather up the liquid of her

last breath into my hands,
and afterwards stand with my back

to the rain, taking its lashings
without once crying out

without crying out once.
The river looks beyond

says, 'Someone will return
to take her place.'

I come away peeling off
the wet garments of grief,

turn my pockets inside out.
Two days later they find her

mangled and silenced
in the pulp of the river.

51 Minakuchi

I lie back and try not to think
of August 6, 1945,
rather observe the pine plumes,
the blue hills of Kyoto.

Women sit in the sun peeling gourds
and hanging the ochreous flesh
from scaffolds. The wind blows the door
open, bombs yet to fall.

Winter welters in my blood.
I think I'm on the Sea of Japan,
it's that bitter cold. People interrupt
me – mother's voice: *One must
always think of others first.*
Like her I now wear sensible shoes.

I watch the twig-carriers
making and mending, heard
the cuckoo this morning.

52 Ishibe

Night plummets as it does on the plain,
mist ambles through woods.
Only the tips of the mountain, grey
for a while, and the sea in the distance,
stretching its vast empty limbs.
Hiro stands and watches
the colour drain from the day.
Some will make it.
Some won't.

Michi ni mayotte shimaimashita

Then light from an inn trips into the street,
dancers let what comes
go. Others leave the little show,
walk towards the acid blue horizon.

She greets him with a cup of rice wine

It will be a radiant night.

You're just one among many
who vanished.

53 Kusatsu

Mariko misspent her youth
at the inn of The Cat Who Laughed.

Hirata-gumo weaves his web
across the threshold.

I've been a good girl
gone around the world.

She stays up all night, lies abed
all day while her lust turns grey.

Hiro waits at the bridge
with something to say.

The camellia he gave her
rises up like onryō,

wind thrashes trees
till leaves submit.

I am no longer young.
Pain endures.

Live with it.

54 Ōtsu

It is the nature of the river
to divide. Kneeling at the water's edge
I turn over pale stones.

I am almost never here
in these old prints, but look harder,
closer, and I'm everywhere.

I've attenuated each title
entreated each kanji
until it is able to speak

until I begin to dream
in another language
with no word for loss.

55 Kyoto

At Sanjo Bridge
the hills are swagged in snow,
the river's surface solid,

deceptive. Beneath its weathered
veins a cold current runs
from source to sea.

Temple smoke streams over the bridge,
purifies pilgrims, eyes
fix on the city of dreams.

There is no clear boundary
between memory and imagination,
memory carries a trace

of place, gives us presence
in absence. Imagination
mends the holes.

I let you go, my blue
familiars, cross the bridge
alone.

Glossary

Abunai danger

Agyō Agyō and Ungyō are temple guardians. Their fierce appearance is
 thought to ward off evil. Each is named after a cosmic sound – the
 open-mouthed Agyō utters 'Ah' for birth, while his closed-mouthed
 companion utters 'Un' or 'Om', meaning ending, death.

Ajisai hydrangea

Asa morning; 'asa no fuji' or 'Morning Fuji'

Ayu a sweet-tasting river fish

Daikon large white icicle radish

Daimyō feudal lord

Danchi 'group land' project of public housing built from the 1950s to the
 70s

Dharma the teachings of the Buddha

Edo military capital of Japan under the Tokugawa shōguns. Renamed
 Tokyo after the Meiji Restoration in 1868.

Futon traditional bedding which can be rolled up and stored during the
 day when not in use

Gaijin foreigner

Go a strategic board game for two players, similar to chess

Hato bus Tokyo's tourist bus service

Hirata-gumo a common house spider that carries its prey home, eats it
 there, and then attaches the leftovers to its home

Hokusai, Katsushika renowned figure in 'ukiyo-e'. Lived 1760–1849. One
 of his most famous works is 'The Wave'. Hokusai adopted many
 different pen names; his favourite was 'an old man mad with paint-
 ing', which he used at the end of his life.

Irasshaimase welcome called out to customers entering a shop or restaurant

Jin person or people

Jizō stone statues seen everywhere along the road in Japan. Sometimes a bib is placed on the statue by a grieving parent who has lost a child in the hope that the Buddha will protect the child in the other world.

Jun ken po stone, scissors, paper game played by children

Kago a palanquin

Kano Motonobu a Japanese painter (1476–1559) who tried to capture the beauty of Sakanoshita but, failing in his task, threw his brush into the valley below. The place has the reputation of being too beautiful to paint.

Kameyama 90th emperor of Japan, reigned 1259–74

Kanji Japanese alphabet based on pictograms of Chinese origin

Kimono traditional full-length Japanese garment worn by men and women. Kimono are worn around the body always with the left side over the right (except when dressing the dead for burial) and secured with a belt called an 'obi' at the back.

Kyoto capital of Japan 794–1868

Maiko apprentice geisha

Mansion modern apartment buildings with multiple floors and secured gates

Michi ni mayotte shimaimashita 'I have lost my way'

Mudra hand position of the Buddha where the right hand is raised to the chest, with the palm facing outwards, joining thumb and forefinger. The meaning is 'no fear'.

Namu Amida Butsu Buddhist chant: 'I trust in the Buddha of Immeasurable Light'

Nihonbashi bridge at the centre of Tokyo; starting point of the Tokaido
and the point from which all distances are measured

Nori edible seaweed

Nyubai the beginning of the rainy season

Obasan literally grandmother, but also a term of endearment for old
women

Oden a winter dish consisting of boiled eggs, fish cakes and radish in a
flavoured stock

Onryō a female ghost who can return to the physical world where she was
formerly powerless, but can now exact vengeance on her male lover

Sakura cherry tree

Sanjūsangendō a temple in eastern Kyoto famous for its 1001 statues of
'Kannon'

Shibori the Japanese term for methods of tie-dyeing cloth by binding,
stitching, folding or twisting. 'Arashi' or 'storm shibori' results in a
pleated cloth with a diagonal design suggesting a heavy rain storm.

Soba a thin Japanese noodle made from buckwheat flour either served dry
with 'nori' or in a broth

Tabi a sock with a separation for the big toe

Tanuki Japanese raccoon dog, part of folklore since ancient times, reputed
to be masters of disguise and shape-shifting. Often gullible and
absent-minded. Pottery 'tanuki' often decorate domestic gardens.

Tatami traditional Japanese flooring made of straw

Tengu creature from Japanese folklore with the body of a human and the
head of a bird

Tennin including the female 'tennyo' are spirits in Japanese Buddhism
similar to angels or fairies. As women, they are extraordinarily beau-
tiful, dressed in exquisite colours. 'Tennin' can fly and are depicted
with feathered kimonos called 'hagoromo' or dress of feathers.

Tojimbo cliffs   in Fukui prefecture north of Kyoto on the western coast of
    Japan, a well-known site for suicide

Tokaido   Eastern Sea Road; main road from Edo to Kyoto

Tokonoma   small raised alcove in a Japanese style room where scrolls and
    flowers are displayed

Torii   gateway, especially to a Shinto shrine

Townsend Harris   (1804–78) opened first US consulate in Japan; joined
    the Tokaido at Mishima on his way to meet the shōgun

Ukiyo   the floating world; 'ukiyo-e' means pictures of the floating world.

Washi   Japanese paper made in the traditional manner

Yamabushi Tengu   mountain or forest goblins with the power to change
    shape into animal or human form, enter dreams and speak without
    moving their lips

Yoisho   an interjection similar to 'Heave-ho'

Ⓑ editions

Fergus Allen *Before Troy*
Jonathan Barrow *The Queue*
Andrzej Bursa *Killing Auntie and Other Work*
    (translated by Wiesiek Powaga)
Nancy Gaffield *Tokaido Road*
Stefan Grabiński *In Sarah's House*
    (translated by Wiesiek Powaga)
Gert Hofmann *Lichtenberg & The Little Flower Girl*
    (translated by Michael Hofmann)
Erik Houston *The White Room*
Gabriel Josipovici *Only Joking*
Greg Loftin *Saxon*
David Markson *This Is Not a Novel*
J. O. Morgan *Natural Mechanical*
D. Nurkse *Voices over Water*
Francis Ponge *Unfinished Ode to Mud*
    (translated by Beverley Bie Brahic)
Christopher Reid *The Song of Lunch*
Jack Robinson *Recessional*
Jack Robinson *Days and Nights in W12*
Nicky Singer *Knight Crew*
Elise Valmorbida *The TV President*
Jennie Walker *24 for 3*
Marjorie Ann Watts *Are they funny, are they dead?*

www.cbeditions.com